Of David.

The Lord is my light and my
   salvation; whom shall I
   fear?
The Lord is the stronghold of
   my life; of whom shall I be
   afraid?
When evildoers assail me to
   eat up my flesh,
my adversaries and foes,
   it is they who stumble and
   fall.
Though an army encamp
   against me, my heart shall
   not fear;
though war arise against me,
   yet I will be confident.
One thing have I asked of the
   Lord, that will I seek after:
that I may dwell in the house
of the Lord
   all the days of my life,
to gaze upon the beauty of the
   Lord and to seek Him in his
   temple.
For he will hide me in his
   shelter in the day of trouble;
he will conceal me under the
cover of his tent; he will lift me
high upon a rock.

And now my head shall be
   lifted up above my enemies
   all around me,
and I will offer in his tent
   sacrifices with shouts of
   joy;
I will sing and make melody to
   the Lord.
Hear, O Lord, when I cry aloud;
   be gracious to me and answer
   me!
You have said, "Seek my face."
   My heart says to you, "Your
   face, Lord, do I seek."
Hide not your face from me.
Turn not your servant away in anger,
   O you who have been my help.
Cast me not off; forsake me not, O
   God of my salvation!
For my father and my mother have
   forsaken me, but the Lord will
   take me in.
Teach me your way, O Lord, and
   lead me on a level path because
   of my enemies.
   Give me not up to the will of
   my adversaries;
   for false witnesses have risen
   against me, and they breathe out
   violence.

Psalm 27:1-12 (ESV)

For all those with heart.

INTRODUCTION 7

LOVE, LUST,
& LONGING 11

GRIEF, REFLECTION,
& REPENTANCE 59

ADVENTURE, NATURE,
& THE CREATOR 91

I simultaneously hold two difficult beliefs - that poetry is difficult, therapeutic, and oftentimes painful to write; and that poetry must be published. To keep hidden the pieces of our souls that we've found a way to decipher would be entirely unjust to those still fumbling around in the dark. For all who've wrestled their own conscience (and I'd venture so far as to say that qualifier encompasses you, the holder of a poetry book), the understanding that dawns in the midst of pain, love, or euphoria is momentous. To finally hold tightly the reins of your own feelings after years of processing and hoping for healing is a gift of God. In the stress of waiting, we can take refuge in the words of King David:

"My sacrifice, O God, is a broken spirit; a broken and contrite heart
You, God, will not despise."
Psalm 51:17 (ESV)

The poetry contained in these pages ranges dramatically. Much of it was written within the last three years, but a fair amount is drawn from many years before that. Chronologically, these poems are evidence of a young man's cycle through sin, repentance, growth, and back into the never-ending war with his flesh. I have ordered the poems *nearly* chronologically within their respective chapters, but I feel as if presenting them at face value would have a different effect than I desire with publishing this work.

My desire with this book you're holding is that you would echo the words of David in Psalm 51, "My sacrifice, O God, is a broken spirit..." These words have left my mouth many times, and have been spoken in my mind even more than that. Ultimately, I believe these are the best words anyone can find themselves speaking, despite the dismal circumstances required to bring most of us to this point.

You see, I've been a man of faith my entire life, but this journey of using poetry to list, on paper and phone screen, my lowest lows and my highest highs has, in a sense, documented a journey from self-reliance and the worship of the created to the worship of The Creator. The one who created heaven and earth, who created you to hold the complexity of thought in order to have the reaction you are currently having to these words. We as artists must acknowledge the ultimate artist - the designer of language, the painter of the skies, the mastermind behind sound itself. To leave Him unannounced is to resign Him to the undertones of the work, and I believe that just as no life can ultimately flourish apart from a true belief and trust in Jesus Christ, so it is with the creative works of men.

In this spirit, I present to you the innermost workings of the human mind – as fleshly, visceral, and true as they come – and leave all glory to the one true God:

"To him who is able to keep you from stumbling and to present you before his glorious presence without fault and with great joy — to the only God our Savior be glory, majesty, power and authority, through Jesus Christ our Lord, before all ages, now and forevermore! Amen."

Jude 24-25 (NIV)

I want to walk across America. Anywhere in the world I could want to go, my feet could take me. That is my ultimate wish, and where I think I can find God. Earth, Asphalt, Concrete, or gravel underfoot, and the world ahead. I could survive on whatever I could eat like handouts, purchased food, MRE's, or whatever else. I could have a water filter and a backpack big enough for it all. As the weather would change, so would I. I must have a reason to long for such an escape, but so far, it has shown only to God. Let me find balance, and let me find myself.

Brett

the Rain

For Them

For the looks of admiration
the sparkle in a kid's eye as a hero runs past.

For the contrast of a hard
freezing forest floor and
her
comforting caress that drives out loneliness.

For the young and bright faces,
7 opposite each other,
eyes searching souls and souls making goals
in hopes they come home above the luggage.

For them.

LOVE, LUST, & LONGING

Bleed

Until the earth moves and the dawn breaks,

Until words fail and sight fades,

I will bleed this love onto paper as proof for all to see.

Lay With Me

Lay with me on that driveway one last time

Stare into my eyes once more and

I swear to God

In one breath

You'd see all those years I've dreamt of us

A galaxy of hope and faith compressed into one moment

Spent lying on hot cement

Hollywood Moment

It rained that night

As if I needed another Hollywood moment

It rained that night we kissed on your driveway
Three years it took me to get that kiss
It was overcast when I asked you to give me a try and you said we should go for it

Three years it took to get that chance

We laid on the hood of my car with only the stars and warm air of a summer night as our company when I told you my biggest fears and you told me yours
Three and a half years it took me to tear down those walls
The autumn sun was just disappearing under a golden sky laced with hues of pink and blue when
I said "I love you" and you said you loved me too
Four years it took before I dared utter those words
When a veil was torn between us you laughed and hugged me. You said you loved me more than I could imagine.
You said a whole lot of things.
I walked into that coffee shop and my heart hurt from seeing you again and knowing we couldn't be. Knowing you were already with him.
From knowing 5 years was gone before I saw the rug flying out from under me
It rained that night you said we couldn't be friends
It rained that night I saw you for the last time It rained and I just stood there as you drove away

As if I needed one last Hollywood moment.

Her

I'm not a warrior, but

give me a sword and I'll fight for Her.

Break in the Static

It's the sound of the morning

The feeling when the breeze stops and the whole world goes quiet

It's the gentle kiss of sunlight

The warmth you've waited all winter for

It's the flowers coloring the sides of the trail

The sweet harmony of rocks and dirt under my boots

It's the moment between songs

The radio stops, and my mind sings of you

Ruminations in the Mind of a Horny College Kid

How much of my heart must I pour out to you before you notice me when you're not horny? So much of this, so much of us is me running around doing everything for you when I know
that all I'll get in return is acknowledgment whenever you're bored of your other friends
But for some reason I persist
I refuse to be accustomed to this backseat affair
This absent minded, offhand love
Because although I know you're worthy of my attention,
I know full well I'm worthy of yours
Your words whisper reassurance to me and I hate coming to you with these worries because they always sound like bitching but your actions scream apathy towards my efforts to make us work
I've dealt with this before, but I don't want to just leave you. I can't just let you go like I did her because you are the cement, filling a hole in my heart I wasn't even aware of
I know you're scared to make anything work and so am I but there isn't a day that passes that I don't feel a longing for something bigger, something more permanent than this cork-stopper-love I keep for the constant flow of blood from my chest.

California

Why do your hairs seem different from others?

Each strand separate yet following the same

Uniform motion down your neck

With your small rebel strand laying

Like a kiss on your cheek.

Do you think of me in your sleep?

The One

A response to the question "how do you know she's the one?" It's a process

It starts with a look

A casual flick of her eyes to yours
Makes the rest of the conversation
Happening around you
Fade away, disappear
But it only lasts an instant The sights and sounds of the world come rushing back and you wonder if you were in a coma or under a spell
It moves to a smile

Her teeth flash
Her eyes squint
She laughs

Your stomach jumps You smile in return but you know a millionaire couldn't put on a better display of fireworks than what you just witnessed.
Her eyes get deeper, and colors appear. The patterns get more intricate every time you blink. Your forehead and hers eat together as her eyes read you the most beautiful sonnet you'll ever hear. You start to notice the way her hair seems to come alive with fire in the sunlight.
The way her shoulders hunch forward when she's engrossed in the task at hand. You hear her voice in the next room when she's across the world. Your ears can't escape what they love the most.
You love her.
Muttered in a dark room in low tones with little clothes to your body But you'd stay that way forever if that's what you had to do to be with Her.

You love her.

Spoken softly but the words cut through the air of the car, the sound of the road and radio that she can't help but sing to.

You love her.

Your heart uses your mouth in a fumbling attempt to put words to what you feel when she looks up from her book for the first time in 20 minutes.

She loves you.

Your heart reassures you when doubt creeps in and insecurities tie your mind to a chair for the slideshow that's been on replay since the last time you said that word.

But she's worth it.

The pattern of the freckles on her face is engraved in your mind
And you wouldn't have it any other way.
The tenacity of her spirit ensnares you daily. Her fiery passion only adds to the fire inside you.

The way she pushes you to be better in every way has you thanking God for her
Every
Single
Day.
In the end, I guess you really know she's the one
When you don't know how she couldn't be.

Your Side of the Bed is So Cold Now

Do you remember that motel in Little Rock?

I love that memory so much That I want to erase it.

I want to wipe all those memories of spiritual connection

Of loose lips locked together

Of two bodies intertwined

Of two people who fucking loved each other

Because it was so beautiful

It made me hold you higher than myself,

Under the impression that maybe one of these days

This emotional suppression would stop,

And we would end up

At a little motel in Little Rock

For the rest of our dimly lit lives

One Day

One day we won't have to dream,
Never again will we be let down by
Empty promises or broken words

Daring to approach
All that could stand in our way
You and I will be a roaring fire, one day

Whisper

I was ready for you

To hear me whisper

"I love you."

For the rest of

Our life

Echoes

Why can I see the fire in your eyes
But not in her heart
I want that ability to see beauty not to be my downfall
I want love
To love you
But I know that I don't love
At least not like I should
    If I could
I know that the whole world would be on fire
And I'd write a poem
With the flickering reflection of all that I never desired, casting shadows
That create more depth than this shallow kind-of love
That doesn't run any deeper than the impression of
Bare bodies on my mattress
Or the way my floor feels itself being hit by your sundress
And I'd much rather disregard morals and just watch you undress
But I wouldn't be able to live with that constant duress,
A tug and pull
Of something much stronger than my hormones
The one who made the looking glass that becomes distorted
Every time the shades are drawn
And we fall right back into the same groove on the bed
That's starting to get too comfortable and deep
That the voices outside
Are now only echoes

Playing Memories Like VHS Tapes

Dear God, please freeze this moment

I plead

We will never need more than this love

Defined by bodies intertwined under blankets

Fed by the warmth of the sun brightening the cold living room

Through those cheap blinds

With knowledge of the frigid world outside

And inside

But no room to heed it we just needed each other

My concentration only broke

From the sound of your laugh that awoke a love inside me that I had

forgotten for God only knows what reason

I saw the phone recording the silly reactions

Your precious giggles

Of which memories I couldn't even sell for the life I'd always dreamed of

We weren't there, and we both knew deep down

We never would be

But dear God, please freeze this moment.

Please God, don't let me forget the love that encompassed

every unknowing second

To Be Loved

The crisp winter sunlight

On crimson brick turned brown

Matches the setting of

Dormant maple and ash around

The contrast of stone and wood

Telling stories of frozen mornings and solar-powered productivity

brought with the afternoon

The road noise carries better

Here in the cold

I drag out memories of each breath

Suspended in time

As if God said "These ones are precious."

As if the earth said "Behold what you have been given."

The rush from warmth through cold to warmth through cold

Reflects the patterns of our lives

Searching for love through despair

To love through anguish

To love through pain

To love through hope

To feel the cold creeping through layers of cloth only

reminds us to never stand still

Reminds us

We only want to be loved.

Morning Whispers

A room full of rough men
Surrounded by fighters
Brothers
Steel will, Iron strength
My mind can only replay

You

Tender words, warm skin on skin, climax
overtaking us both in time we lost
with words we hope to hear until we die
"I love you" we whisper
Our love knows more than this –
It knows God
Look up and

Back to the war

Flowers through the Moon

With every breath of chilled air that expands my chest

With every crunch of these dead leaves underfoot

With every dormant vine, bush, and tree lining this wooded path

I can feel your body pulled into shape with mine

The curves of our hips aligning like the stars

The strength of your shoulders and back gently enveloped by mine

Your velvet lips brush the back of my hand as our fingers

Entwine against your chest

With every breath

With every step

With every path

I am reminded of your dreams to have your progress and imperfections

Painted in vibrant color

Displayed on your back, twisting into and between the

Phases of the moon that my

Lips have touched so tenderly

I want so desperately to be even but a bloom

Though I pray to God that

I can be the vine

Bootprints

The dead trees wake at your touch.

These green desert leaves illuminate as you walk past.

The sand is calm beneath your feet, but the rocks stir in your gaze.

These iron-rich canyon walls nod in approval of your approach.

Your heart wakens the tiny animals.

Red dirt settles underfoot, content with its benevolent monarch.

The sun makes known every kiss with which it has graced your skin and
    I am in awe.

You are the goddess of these canyons
    The queen of the morning light.

Love Me Eyes

You lean into me

Your hips tilt forward

To feel

I feel

Thoughts left 5 hours ago

On the brink of sleep

With one head tilt

And those "love me" eyes

Your lips locked mine

In an instant we threw our premonitions away

Clothes and cares hit the ground

Whilst decisions are made instantly

That the feeling of your small rib cage in my rough palms

That the feeling of your thin hips under my calloused fingers

That the feeling of your body tilted into mine

That the feeling of copulatory whispers;

Only millimeters separating lips and lips, lips and ears

Meant more than morals

That to hold one another

Was more important than to uphold an image

To cherish was more important than to fake needs

Your needs were mine

And the pulsing of your body moving in time

Blue Dawn Light

The blinds filter

Blue dawn light

Barely blanketing the vast

Array of softly distinguishable freckles

Blessing the bridge of your small nose

This last-second sleepover

As a romantic more-than-strangers

Kind of time

Spent under covers

Eyes not closed

Brains under the drugs that are

Hips, legs intertwined

With lips on cheeks, necks, lips

Tasting the blue hue

Letting your freckles fall into my mouth

Your whispers grace my longing ears

Your panting slipping into my mind long after

I've rolled down that gravel driveway

Gray-Blue

Your eyes speak many words

I've heard them deep in the twists of my mind

I've read them in neon color brightly displayed across your iris

That gray-blue

I've never read before you

That night

Your eyes said

"I love you."

Hearts Longing

Our eyes speak and know

      what our hearts long we'd say.

Make Love Not War

Wind through pines
Mimicks distant road noise
Cool morning walk

Follows a nearly sleepless,
Dream-full night

Warm sun now thaws tight muscles
Frigid from the forest floor

A lazy breeze now makes
Woodwinds out of the trees

A perfect setting for my heart to remember these people
I've been blessed by

My heart is left wanting for
Your Love Alone.

Dove

A gradient sky

Blessed by thoughts of you

Tensions could be cut

Closed eyes and controlled breaths

Fix my thoughts, remind me of you

Anger released to Him

Love refocused to you

Control relinquished, floating north

Coming undone, unraveled, unwound, unbound

Changing from red to orange to gray to purple to black

From hate to love

Only possible above

Blessed by the gift of a dove.

I Forget Where We Were

My head in your hands,
pressed to your chest with
only thoughts interrupting skin.

The Back Porch

Six hours.

Give me six hours. This frigid gentle wind challenges the warmth of the sangria in my stomach and the layers on my skin.

How would I begin?

We'd sip hand in hand and hand on face and lips on cheeks
and hands on clothes
Chilled digits sliding under warm fabric for the sweet release of
skin on skin
However and whenever and wherever it might begin.
We can make this moonlight hum
With the sound of our bodies and hearts moving in rhythm
like a drum beating
And an indie folk band playing
Strumming chords on the cold wind blowing
Making muscles shiver and skin retract
Our bodies and minds and hearts in a silent and momentary contract
To never contact the outside world again.

There is only your heart beating in time with mine.

There is only the sweat now freezing to our skin as we lay in the aftermath of hormones and emotions, unbound by foolish worldly constructs like time and place and thought.
There is but naught that might replace the lack of speech in my mouth when I attempt to comprehend each gentle corner and sharp curve that defines the face that is, for these fleeting seconds, my entire reality.
There is only the smell of your self covering my self in fluids which mentioned bring roses to cheeks.

There is only your stormy sea eyes ceding their tiny island of earthen color to the archipelago of evergreen and ocean waves that comprise my own iris'.

There is, for two more breaths, just us.

There are just the sounds of red-haired, barefoot, curious, fearless children running through our front yard behind you while you tend the flowers at the base of our front porch.
There is just a gate swinging shut behind me, and a blue roof kissing my peripheral vision while my pupils contract at the sight of weapons laid down, and a single braid care-freely falling down your back.

There is only heavy breathing.

There is only moonlight kissing my tight back and
your attentive breasts.
There are only the coming winter winds,
falling across our skin.
There is only warmth inside.
There is only love on our back porch.

Evening Pines

Golden hour rays

Weave through evening pines

Heat from this hot day

Leaves in waving lines

I can't find words to say

To describe these thoughts of mine

I yearn for days we'll play

Losing track of time

Hand in hand we'll lay

Beneath the evening pines

Whatever come what may

Until the end of time

Pillow Math

I wish your head was on the pillow next to mine

And my job was asinine:

To count the freckles on your face

Here in the dark.

I wouldn't dare leave out a mark.

When Will I See You Again

She's a goddess
In the afternoon light
Her auburn hair catches fire
From the rays of sun
Filtered through the cheap white plastic blinds
The dark freckles on marble skin
Are like careful dots from a paintbrush
Only solidifying her place in your mind
As a renaissance masterpiece
Her confident curves
Accented by swathes of cloth and light
Are a canvas on viewing you couldn't bear but delight
In the fore and backhand strokes of the paintbrush
God used to place her in front of you
The way her locks grace her shoulders and back
They fall with such poise - they must know the power they hold
As she looks back to see your face
Her eyes hold yours with a beauty so deep
Magnifying the light from between the shades
Fluorescently, incandescently blue
Staring right at you
Now you understand the paintings and statues
She's a goddess

The Little White Flowers

As we talk
You're reading this book
I've placed in your hands
You read aloud and Words I know well fall on my ears.
I've bled the words
That fill these pages for years
And will for years to come
There's illustrations too and
One of them looks just like you
Only
There's flowers where your face should be and covering every page
From the day I looked at you, and you me
Filled with purples and whites and blues
Like the flowers I might have prayed for you
To put in my hair, and you did.
And I you.
Like a projector outline falling in line with the real picture
Until suddenly it snapped
And there you were
A woman with a heart for the Lord
Reading this book
I've almost died writing
More than once
I couldn't help but adore
You on first sight
I knew that you were for me
And I for you
With these little white flowers in our hair
I dare anything to stand in our way

I Forgot Something in Your Car

Why does it have to be like this
Why do I want you?
An even better question:
Why do I feel like I shouldn't?
Is this guilt? Is this shame? Or is this the spirit who loves me and looks out for me? Who wants the best for me? Because it sure as hell doesn't feel like He wants the best for me when I lock eyes with you. When I hold you for two straight minutes, just "saying goodbye."
I'd rather not.
I'd rather not let go
I'd rather pull you in closer
Closer than we'd dare allow ourselves to speak out loud
But as close as our hearts know is fitting.
Letting our hearts and bodies
Duke it out to determine the best standing
Sounds better than turning away and grasping for a phrase to say that isn't
"I love you."
or
"Fucking kiss me already."
A phrase that quenches the starving thirst that has been dominating every second of today, dominating every thought when I dare to stare at your body and let your heart reach my ears instead of pushing them deeper and deeper to fight this feeling that comes so freely and strongly
This feeling
It's a fire, catching the cotton stuffed in my ears and burning it quicker than I can load more in, opening my brain to hear what my heart speaks when you grab my hat and
Don my hoodie
I carry an extra of both because I wouldn't dare tell you no
No, That would deprive me of my favorite sight.
One that upon reaching my eyes makes me think I just might fucking
Love you.

God, define that word in my soul
Before I give in to this tug and pull
That says our clothes need thro-

Fuck it, we're both grown
Can't we make this bed shake with
The phrases our eyes have been silently exchanging for a month?
God save me from myself
I can't possibly make the right decision
I'll need a division of your strongest angels
To pull my mind off this
Give me concision
And Lord, my God, give me the
Love You want.

Her Words

The air around her glows spiritually
No wind or light or lack thereof can diminish it
Only accentuate or increase it
Her skin is covered in the blood she's shed
Not as a warning
Not because she forgot to wipe it off
But as a trophy from the battles she's won
And the fountain outpouring from her heart comes
Not from her own strength, only that of the Spirit
Her living is a testament to His Greatness
Her words are calculated
Her words are meaningful
Her words are deliberate and piercing to the core of who you are
Behind closed doors slowly and deliberately being undone
But not in the way that makes you run
No fight or flight, just freeze
You're subject to assist her words in finding
Whatever her mind and heart are searching for
You throw up a wall and
She opens it like a door
Peruses the halls
Of your inner spirit
Careful not to touch anything
Only hear it
She has no ill-intent
Her heart rings true
Through the Spirit known by the both of you
You're calm, terrified to relinquish the sovereignty of your solitary mind.
The questions slowly falling from her lips
Dare you to exist
Just as you are

06 March

Your brown hair

With the tinge of red you hate

Burns while you stand there

On our two-day date

A Capital "L"

Your eyes
Make a bed for me
Of pine boughs
Ripped from a live tree
A couple minute walk from the place
We laid our tents at
Just close enough to the creek
We splashed across
That darkness-turned-lamp-light
Instantly showed something
I was scared of
Something I Loved
The thoughts of leaves slapping bare legs
Trailblazing through lush brush
Not waiting until the sun goes down
To share hushed words
That fuel our hearts
That seem like lucid dreams
And seeing the touch of brown on
Forests of green
Is tearing me apart at the seams to not say
I Love you.
I can't possibly think of a world that's not true.
The way we knew
Upon first breath in the presence of me
And I, you
That the fruit, I've struggled to bear
But it's there
Fruit, singular
Love Joy Peace Patience Kindness Gentleness and Self Control

I can't think of a time I wouldn't want those eyes to have a hold on me.
I can't think of a future I wouldn't want filled with
Love and laughter and you and I

Pushing after Christ. THAT Love.

With the capital "L"
There's no way it's the same.
It's not like the others
It hasn't taken over my brain
It's blessed me
Day and night the same
Whenever I think of a word
Or your name
I'm brought back to Him.
To His grace, His mercy
His wisdom, His blessings
Poured forth onto the children
He Loves
With a capital "L"

The Willow Crown

I feel now

As if I've cried for the innocence of the many

And never my own

Before you built me a throne

And adorned me with a Willow Crown

Your North Dakota Poem

I think we have it
Pink toenails and Chaco's
At a picnic table in
Nowhere, North Dakota
There's nothing more that
I wish for, but the presence of Him
And you draw me there
I'm reminded by every red hair
On my denim jacket

Awoken

I wake

To you

The warm blue glow of the sunrise

Puts your breath in my heart

And your hairs in my sight

I won't ever get enough

Of you in this morning light

I Can't Remember

I can't for the life of me remember the words
you cried to me that night.
But I do remember
The way your head lay on my chest
Bare, every article of clothing
Lay bare on the floor
And your heart spoke more and more
Of everything you've ever wanted
Of how you dared not feel adored
For risk that it might be real,
A chance it might hurt once more
So you cried there,
Tears streaming in the dark
Thinking of him who'd left a mark
And wondering why I never did
I never said I loved you, but now I think
I did
Love the pain you'd been through
Because it let me be there for you
We'd finish tangling the sheets
Once I'd finally organized them again
And we'd return to this spot
Slightly damp forehead on a slightly sweaty chest
Legs, feet, hips, and hearts and all the rest
Entangled and ensnared
With love we'd never dared call
Love because we knew it wasn't
We knew it couldn't be
At least you knew it couldn't
Not from me.

Of Lust

The drinks

To cloud those loud voices inside
There have to be drinks

The eyes

Piercing soul from pierced soul, telling
It always starts with the eyes

They do what they do to say it has to be love
It must be love, otherwise there's no name for
them except manipulators, animals, sinners.

Their confidence was fine a minute before they sat in the car, but now
they smell their perfume and them and they're nervous, so they
comfort.

It's weak circular reasoning to get their
hands on soft rounded areas; to get the
other under sheets the first time they
meet.

To get the other to elicit the noises they need, but they're not their name.
They don't need to be, and they don't remember it anyways.
They hold their hands, and they hold back; they're both soliciting more
than they're consoling, both taking more than they're giving
simultaneously.

The drinks cloud their mind but they remember the words that made the last one squirm in pleasure; they remember the moves that made the last one finish, so they use those in a desperate attempt to feel something they could think of as love.

They finish and kiss then reverse the order, desperately and drunkenly reaching for a shred of solace in the hope that the best they've ever had really is that in every way and feeling and future.

Their eyes speak and know what their hearts think, but the only thing that matches is their domineering and their submission.

They'll share the room for a night or maybe more, but they'll never share more than a framework of themself with the other; they'll never share more than a squeaking bed frame and pillow under the hips.

Fluid motions and fluid moving means nothing to being fluent within souls.

Head on Chest

The beads of sweat on our bare skin
Combine with our foreheads touching
My breathing slowly gets deeper
I feel your heart
Come forth from your chest
Bare, exposed, as our bodies and feelings always are
When we come to this room
It holds me
Your capacity for compassion
Always astounded me
But I don't think I ever comprehended that
you knew exactly what this was
I played you for a fool letting me use you
But you wanted nothing more;
To be used meant you could help another
Meant your heart could leave its sharp, defended hiding place
Beneath your clothing and rib cage
To sweep out cobwebs and stitch up wounds
My lips and forehead would lay on the center of your chest in guilt
And you'd soak me up
In my mess you'd start cleaning without movement or touch
Brushing thoughts aside, somehow your heart touching mine
Every time with no words or whispers
Every time, with no words, even whispers
I'd come for the bare sheets on the bed
You'd come to continue slowly making sense of this mess
That encompassed my every breath

Sunlight Rays

Sunlight is different Because of you
Brighter and clearer
Making colors more full
It creates clear breathes
It clears mind and soul
To be able to feel
The depth of its rays
Seeing the ways
This sunlight plays
I'd love to see like you
For the rest of my days

Unanswered Questions from Apartment 5043

Why does your body on mine Smell of late summer and warm regret?
Why does my body on yours
Taste of the third story bedroom and
August light through dusty shades?
Why do I feel pleasantly bereft here lacking your copulatory whispers?
Why do our legs interweaved sing a glorious chorus of sin that we ignore?
What would it take to make things right?
What would it take to

smell the monsoons in late summer.
taste golden hour in the August Afternoon.
hear silence, here. feel, not cast off?

What would it take to return to what could be?

GRIEF, REFLECTION, & REPENTANCE

19 February

I'm slowly writing away all of the memories

    that shine so bright

        they burn.

You Died

You died.
Sure other people will say you've just moved on, but they haven't known you for this long.
When you laughed then looked away that night, telling me I know you better than anyone else, you meant it and I could tell.
I know you're dead.
I know you're dead because I looked at the old pictures tonight and after 45 minutes of remembering, the luminescence of your face and the brilliant sparkle in your eyes and your teeth showing the way they do when you laugh really hard; the way your nose would scrunch and your eyes would squint when I told a bad joke but you'd crack up anyways

My phone died.

I was unplugged from the virtual reality where you were still here and I wasn't afraid of loving anything
I was ripped from those memories and placed in the harsh light of my room at 3a.m.
I was placed in the setting I didn't want the setting
I was trying so hard to escape
This world without you.
People will say you've moved on
"People change,"
You haven't changed though, you've died.
I know because your face is gray.
I know because your eyes no longer sparkle
I know because I don't see your teeth when you smile
I know because your eyes are wide open and your nose smooth
I know because I saw you I didn't recognize you or you me...
You died.
And I cried that night until I realized that I wasn't just crying for you.

I Put a Rose on My Wrist

I watched you grab anything close to you and tear it down
I was with you the whole way and I did the exact same thing.
As we struggled to escape that pit
I saw the red lines on your arm
I saw the shadows in your eyes
I saw the color fade from your cheeks
I saw you cry, I saw you fall apart
And I loved you.
So I changed the narrative of despair, and I used this hole we dug
To plant this hurt and watch it grow
Into a version of us more beautiful than I could imagine.
I sketched the lines on my wrist
I shaded the curves and breaks
I splashed the hues of your cheeks onto the leaves
I painted the color of your eyes into each precious petal
I planted hope for us, right there in my arm.
I put a rose on my wrist
So you wouldn't ruin yours.

The Room

I would sit around the corner
You would talk to me
Bare the bones of social stigmas and laugh them out of existence
I miss that
I don't miss you, but I miss *that*
More than you can know, because now
I'm only honest when those bones are shown air and
Lord knows I've yet to see them bare
Since you
Sharing that small room
That twin bed
That place we called home for but a short while
Gave me such hopes that we could see
Another day together where we wouldn't fight
We would drown our spite in the face of the light
We gained from a promise
That never was said
Only eager mutterings vaguely resembling
The specifics of our contract set out before those mornings
That we never spent together
It's felt like years without you
And I think that's a good thing
But nothing can tear away this caring thread that was sewn into the
Fray of my heart, surrounding the hole that was
Shot clear through by that love.
She's here now, but I can't
I can't let her in
I can't let her in fast enough
To wipe these memories of 228 square feet
Clean off my mind.

Time Machine

I long to go back in time.
Back to when the comfort of a warm stomach and a blurred reality
weren't my daily aspirations
Back to when my feelings could take much more than a whisper and
whiskey was watered down because a clear mind was preferred.
But now I no longer have your intoxicating presence
Your poisonous body left me frail, your pernicious love clawed a hole in
my heart
So I fill the gap
With a fluid that expels fear
With a drink that makes me fun
With a solution for my seemingly ever-dampened personality
With a cure for my loneliness
More than a year of my life was yours and I don't say it was wasted, no, that
would make it seem like I didn't want you to take me for a ride and
make a man out of me, like I didn't want you to fuck me up
No, nothing but potential was wasted in those years
Now I'm afraid.
Afraid that what I once was will come back upon me and make me
whole again
Leave the gap filled with someone or something that isn't you
Someone or something that isn't this
Because I've come to like this hole I've dug myself into It's growing on
me in most senses in fact
I've come to love it so much I wouldn't mind an escape here
6 feet deep In mind numbing liquid
Oh how I long to go back in time.

Shotgun Slideshow

The rain pelted the windshield
The gentle roar of the road was almost
As deafening as the silence from the passenger seat
It was as if a projector was flipping through memories
At the speed of my accelerating heartbeat
But skipping pieces and overlooking glances and
Dismissing piercing eyes
Still I felt them all the same, impaling my heart, invading my brain, and crushing the breath from my lungs
As I hoped to see any real version of you in that seat but there wasn't a single one.
Every memory of your sleepy self
Flickering through like an old motion picture
Curled up with your socks and blanket on because of how cold I kept the car
You'd always lecture me on how important sleep was but
I knew the more I closed my eyes the less I'd see
Your peaceful resting face and I loved that.
I felt God in that.
You never did feel Him.
I love you so much it breaks my heart to think that the reason we failed was because I wouldn't preach to you, I wouldn't grow with you,
I couldn't help but wonder what we'd be if we had just
Believed.

Sunflower Sundress

There has to be more than this
Sun-through-the-closed-shades
Kind of time spent
It's a behind-closed-doors kind of loitering that's lacking in coverings
With a head on your chest,
Watch the sunset paint the clouds
Through the cracks in the blinds
Shining brighter colors than my blindness to moral corruption
Could ever produce
Wonder where and how and when
This could ever be better
This could ever fulfill the promise that was made so long ago
The promise made just seconds before
Can I ever set my spirit free
Can I ever escape this heart wrenching, self-deprecating, flesh pleasing,
Counterfeit kind of compassion

A.D.D.

I can't help but think how this

post-love pizza tastes just like

my parent's disappointment.

Map Dot

I can't go back to Amarillo, Texas

George Strait couldn't have known

The pain I see on that map dot

Centered on that hat

I'll never go back

Even just driving through

Gives me visions of the tent

Pitched in front of her car

At that KOA on the side of I-40

We thought we were free

As only young love can be

Now cast to sea

Never to see

Amarillo, Texas again

Gray Hairs

What am I running from?

A night of sunset rowboats to the middle of the lake
A walk down the pier
Camping on the gravel riverbank and falling asleep
With her head on my chest
To walk the brick streets of a small-town downtown
And her hand in mine

Log cabin front porch sunset complete with rocking chairs and gray hairs
Nothing between us but love sobered by experience and
Strengthened by time
What more could I ask for
But... I can't get there

What am I always running from?

Chasing the sunset and stars on a midnight clear
Following the feeling of cold morning air sipping gas station coffee
Pursuing the untainted, wild desert sunrise
Always pressing to the satisfaction of a summit
Seeking companionship but abandoning my best chance of it

Trusting these rust-colored canyon walls and river clay
Will guide me towards the place my head might lay
Forever, in the presence of another.

"Blessings"

Why do my blessings go so counterbalanced?

Why have I been blessed so many ways in the body and spirit if only for my mind to leak and pour from the overflow of black tendrils always reaching from dark to grab more evil and lay it as the foundation of action inside my heart?

I sing praises to the Lord only hours after I've rejected him entirely for

Pain.
Violence.
Blood.
Love.
Lust.
Touch.

My disgusting blood flows heavy through these veins
with each pulse of
my repulsive heart.

Trust

There's poetry in the confidence
The dangerous vulnerability
Of a stranger's head on your chest
A stranger's hands on yours
With nowhere to go
In the name of pleasure-seeking
In the name of nervous excitement
They cry "yes, don't stop"
Because they don't remember your name.
You remember theirs, but this isn't a memory game
You'll dump that knowledge in a few hours anyways
Because longevity isn't something you're after
In fact
You're after the feelings
The approval
The gasping
The admiration
The praise
The admonishment
The eyes closed remembering of times with those we truly love
The pure, poetic, unadulterated
Trust.

Silence

Open your eyes.
No birds.
Silence.
Turn your head, a 2-day beard scratches the cheap throw pillow on an old couch.
Gray light filters through the blinds.
Open them.
It only makes the shade of gray lighter.
Sit up and the couch shifts loudly.
Silence.
Not even the digital clocks tick.
Walk over to the bathroom, let out the regrets from the night before.
The bathroom door squeaked a little louder, he's up now.
Minimal words exchanged, mostly looks and mutual pains.
Tie your shoes in
Silence.
He locks the front door behind you both without words.
Boots grip concrete and frigid air quietly burns your nostrils.
One thousand, one hundred and four steps later. Throw the gift card wrapper in the neighbor's trash bin.
I hope this has money on it.
Footsteps on cold pavement are accompanied by the hospital construction crew starting up for the day.
Silence at a crosswalk.
Dead avenues reflect the sky. Grab your coffee off the counter and thank the barista.
One thousand, three hundred and seventy-six steps later.
A little more uphill on the way back.
Silence at the kitchen table.
Hug and leave.
You're not a good influence.
Walk to the car, past an insecure college kid.
Silence.
The motor growls softly to fight the ice enveloping the car.

Watch the windshield melt, second by second passing but no ticking of the clock.
Don't start.
Silence.
U-turn.
Sub-par graffiti.
Left at the light.
I don't want to fight.
Stare at the busted brake light in front of you.
Silence.
Fill the tank up.
Take a shit in the gas station.
Paper stapled to a telephone pole says a new book just printed.
You finally accept that the dirt on your lucky jacket won't come off without laundry soap.
Pothole.
Road noise.
Silence.
You remember you've been wearing the same gray t-shirt for more than forty-eight hours.
You'll change it later. Roll the windows down to quiet the
Silence.
Get out.
Her name appeared on a cold morning walk
between skyscrapers and scaffolding.
But it was the wrong name.
You loved one but not the other.
You still haven't turned the music on.
Your thoughts are too loud.
The car is silent.
The crunch of stubble under calloused hands.
The way your bodies fit together.
The way she held you.
The way you held her.

Silence.
Please, God, get out.
You just loved the thought of her.
Why does it always have to be sex with you?
Why does it always have to be sex with them?
Stop please I can't take it.
Silence.
The clicking of the car fan.
The interstate traffic.
Another overpass.
The way those jeans hugged her ass.
Fuck.
God, make it stop.
Pothole.
No turn signal.
Silence.
Turn the music on.
Silence.

Published

They published the poem
I wrote about you
It seems strange reading words
I meant for us two
Ink on a page before thousands of eyes
That don't know of our demise
A downfall so tragic and rough
Only made possible by calling a bluff
You had no clue you were running
I'm not sure how I feel
About these words being read
When those thoughts are long dead.

Shower Thoughts

Water overhead

Curtain stuck to skin

Hair drenched and falling Looking down at feet no longer caked in dirt,

sweat, and blood

Steam rises from the drain

Hot water on my skin

Doesn't register as pain

Like what could have been

Zoned Out in the Gym Locker Room

The tiles are a creamy beige, a little bit like her skin.

The way she smiled
All those families walking around
Fathers with children in hand
Mothers showing smiles and giving greetings
Really set you off again
So many smiles
The bright eyes of young mothers
The facade of sternness on the faces of young fathers
Holding children old enough to walk but not old enough to be let go
I wish I didn't know
The way they talked across the pillows at night
But I too was once staring into eyes so full of light
In the dimly lit bedroom so free from spite
That we thought we just might make it to forever
The thoughts of children in your arms just like that
And your hair up in a ponytail
Because you would never dare to fail
To work hard bringing our kids up in love
I miss you deeply
The way she talked to me last night
Showed me I just might have made
Every woman since you a coverup
This wound has been open so long and it's never been sewn up
It's laid open there
Nerves touching cold air
Whenever I see brown hair
With the tinge of red just like yours
Or the way you'd speak behind closed doors
Always reminds me of the amount you'd give to others
Though we stayed poor
Not just your time but your heart and more

You kept an open avenue of love
Outpouring time and effort
But never could manage to be here next to me
Your seat in this car is so cold and lonely
I might as well name it after you
Because the face of everyone who sits in it
Turns into yours in less than a minute
I'm just left trying to finish and move on
But my soul is left wanting for what you'd promised
Though I somehow knew you'd never be able to follow through
I still believed you
And now my heart is filled with grief and pain for what could've been
Every time I see a kid holding their parents' hand
And a wife smiling at her husband
And a husband smiling at his wife
We could've had such a good life
But you were ready to let it go in one day.

"Hey man are you okay?" the beige tiles speak.

"Yeah man, I'm good."

It's been 27 months of staring into the deep.

What's Behind the Shotgun Seat

Thank you for the silence
After screaming
Thank you for standing on the bridge in the early hours of the night and posing as cars went underneath just as we'd seen in the hotel windows from the street side seating at the burger restaurant
Thank you for laughing and calling me names when I spill my insecurities and shortcomings to you
It actually makes me feel better
Whether that makes sense or not
Thank you for driving so I can stare at the skyline while we cross the Cumberland under the warm glow of the stars, the radio, and the streetlights.
Thank you for surprising me by coming to town.
Thank you for taking 10 minutes worth of pictures to preserve our youth and friendship for the many years to come.
Thank you for keeping the radio tuned to a full creek cresting a two-foot drop right before it crosses under the bridge.
Thank you for being my friend, even when I drive myself into a ditch.

Wounded

This wound is so deep

You've spent years fighting the demons that come out of it

With no time or effort left to stitch it back up

But that's what it needs

They're spawning in the festering depths

That can be healed if you tried

But then you'd have to admit it's there

You'd have to admit you've been hurt

You'd have to admit that you weren't stronger than her

You'd have to admit the things she said

Speak them out loud to an understanding

Yet still very

Human

Audience to heal

SSDD

The dirt crunches just the same
The day after rain
As the way the crabgrass grew
Around those patches of cracked mud
The roadside daisies
Bring memories rushing back
The sounds of cicada and killdeer
Echo off the walls of your mind
That's now an empty movie theater
You're the only one
Sitting 12 rows back, center of the chairs
Strapped in
Watching your 8-year-old self run through the same fields thousands of miles and years away
Tripping on chunks of grass
Receiving bee stings and clover honey all the same
Not thinking of how it will impact your brain
In 20 years when you start to feel insane
From the same old mundane shit
To the point that your mind and soul stop like they've been hit by a car
When you're walking in the morning to a waffle house high-bar

Ghosts

The ghosts of every woman I've ever loved

live in my shotgun seat.

Right Field

Let the bottle roll away
It's only a half liter of beer
Because only half of me is there
Watching through a screen
It's better this way, honestly
Because no one can hear my thoughts
Or guess why the tears are falling
At such a beautiful sight
I'm watching in the dim light
Of a phone screen on an empty baseball field
I made my own little lonely home
Out here in right field
But instead of licking snow cones
I'm drowning my neurons to prevent
More tears from falling
I missed it by that much
The summer that every friend I love
Is growing
Is taken from me
I'm left like an 8th grader who moved away the week of graduation
Staring at the grass in right field
And the concrete across the foul line
Except this time
I'm not afraid of the ball
No
I wish a line drive would put my lights out
And the beer has numbed me up enough to
Stare down the stitches and eat it
Just thinking of a lovely wedding
I couldn't even be there to see it

No Sleep

Don't fall asleep
That's when we can't explain
The ethereal space we enter

      It's not nightmares

It's not nearly that bad

      It's worse

Much more passive

      It's weight

Cold and crushing

      Drowned by blaring big band music
      and the smell of Newports

It's the weight of our very flesh

Not lifted by streetlights painting your legs in the shotgun seat
in light then dark
in light then dark
in light then dark
then dark

Out The Window

Dogs got it right
You gotta try this
Head out the window
Sunshine on eyelids
Bleaching your hair
Let go, don't care
Wind blows it all away
The next sunny day,
Soak it in, for every photon it's worth

Marriage Bed

Look her in the eyes desire, longing fear

"Say you'll never leave me."

This is twice now I remember
as my brain rushes back through that string of scenes and feelings
and feelings of touch
heavy breathing became more touching
became heavier breathing became cut ribbons
with scissors we didn't know how to wield
and had no business doing so
again only this time I'm to blame
I'm the one marked skin blackened and charred
wounds barely sewn up through the power of forgetfulness,
not healing
reopened this time not by drinks and mellow music
but hands, legs, eyes, and souls tied together
on another cheap excuse for a
marriage bed.

One Bridge Over

It could've been you

standing illuminated
under the lone sconce lamp shining over
the dark back alley Venetian canal bridge
one street over from mine

but it wasn't.

In The Middle of The Night

Returnfiremake'emhurtboysohSHITjohnson'shitthegroundreturnfirekill'emallgoddamnfuckin'hajjisWax'emthey'llbesorrytheywereeverbornhavetoapologizetotheirmotherinhellstupidfuckin'

MEDIC!

Johnson'sdownhe'stalkingnonsensebleedingrealbadDocheneedshelpwhatareyougonnadoletmehelpItookaCLScourseIcanhelpareyousurethisistheb estwayhe'sstillbleedingheywaitDocPat'sgottaMEDEVAConthewayDocgimmelines3,4,5thebirdneedsitNOWheyishegonnamakeitdocwhat'shedoingheneedshelpweneedaMISTDocwhatthefuckhappenedwhy'dheclosehise yeshe'sgoingunderDocheyyouGOTTAHELPHIMDOC-

Stop.

Watch the ceiling fan spin.
Slow down, breathe out then in
Feel the sweat on your bare chest.
Look to your left and see
Her.
Grab her hand gently, she'll wake up

Slowly

Things will get better.

ADVENTURE, NATURE, & THE CREATOR

Still He Shines

Morning light turns green leaves a fiery emerald
The sound of sunlight cresting mountains
Spoke of love as gentle as a small-town morning

At end of day

The world goes silent
Watch the burning sky fall out of sight
In absence of light

Still He shines

Fiery Sun

The smell of dust permeates the air
Until a soft breeze echoes in your ears
Tousles your hair
Gently brushes the hairs on your left arm
The cicadas drown out the sound of airplanes overhead, this time of year
The jackrabbits are all standing motionless
Heads pointed west.
The cicadas cease to call
The breeze gently leaves, like a friend walking away
After a tender goodbye.

"Let the sun set," the desert says

I can do nothing but comply.

10 March

I found God's peace

In the birds

Perched on trees

Through the road noise

Under the clouds

And over the sunset

Streets of Gold

The carpet
At the base of the
Window is
Worn from
Watching the
White clouds stroll
Thunder clouds roll
Green grass grow
Newborn birds thrown from the nest
Like these dreams that we won't let rest
Until we've come to the floor in front of this window
Enough times that the acoustic tunes and chirps of spring
Match the vibrancy of sunrise and sunset like the thing
That brought us here in the first place
Speculating as if we could absorb this peace through our face,
Pressed to the viewing glass
Soaking in greens and yellows
Blues and reds
Purples and oranges
With faith that they might color our lives one day

But until then
We wear our summer-day-in-LA sunglasses
In hopes that warmer hues will bend our wanting views to
Streets of gold

01 September

Such beauty is found in this column of holy fire.

Hundreds of desperate souls

Pressing the eye of a needle

Flock to the shores

In search of a sanctification that surpasses

Gratification in the forms of

Man, woman, and child alike

Cold Mornings in Old Cars

The thin smoke floating from your lips

in unconsciously even bursts

makes the world stop.

Tousled Hair

There's something to be said
For silence
The utter lack of any forced input the practice of only existing
To absorb
That around you
To feel every breath of cold air expand in your lungs
To embrace the wind roughly caressing your face with every gust
To let your hair go unfixed, carried away
By the designs of nature
To breathe in and feel your soul envigored
To breathe out and feel your heart mature

Sonoran Blood

I was born of the desert
My skin is the pale sandstone of the cliffs
My muscles are the granite faces of the canyon walls
My heart is the limestone formations
My blood is the red clay and
I am rich in nothing but composition

Like the soaring walls that surround the gentle river of Zion
Is my love for the life
Found in sand and sage alike
This soft red clay dyes my intentions
I can't go long but for to mention
The towering mountains
Of the Sonoran
Pieced together from the magma;
The blood of the Kayenta
Overflowing from its time
Onto any willing to listen
To the tales a desert could tell

Worth More

Let His peace last
Fill my untrusting heart
With headstrong and blind
Love
I know my worth by now
My emphatic desire to love
To serenade you with sunsets and songs of promise and emotion
Help to carry the motion
That I am worth more than she would ever be willing to give
And I will not be bought on sale
I've been purchased by the one who invented affection
Nothing can beat His price
Of absolutely and irrevocably

Free

No returns, no refunds, no money back guarantee
That which He loves is me
That love which He can only know
So poorly absorbed yet still adored
By a son who can't get it right
Though I fight
I am so far short of the purchasing power of
His life

The Creek Bend

Rain has been falling but

The sun has now tested the clouds

Birds chirp

This gentle creek excites me

The crisp flow of clear water

Moss filled rock channel

Purifies my

Breath, Soul, Lungs, Mind, Heart

In the midst of toil

Under blood and strength

Let the peace of the Lord through

Nature fill me with a soul like this

Here in His presence

I ask every question my heart could want known

He fulfills me

Garage-Bound Blues

The construction of new
In a soft lime
The colors of spring
Accompanied by birds
Flings me into a frenzy
Of appreciation for a new hue
To the tree limbs
The R&B from the garage
Walks the sun off stage
To the applause of the
Slow-rolling clouds

Hearts and Minds

What brings the peace to this Tennessee air?
There's none like it I have felt before
Through the shimmering light reflecting off the silver-lined clouds,
Something more
The grass more richly green
The blue particularly serene
The wind uniquely keen
All distinctly separate pieces
But all one scene
The ground breathes
The air seethes
The bugs begin to call
Spring, like an overweight drunkard, fell on us all
We are made to roam the halls
Yet, from inside my spirit calls
To free my wrists of the bondage so false
Emplaced by a body with paws
Eager to snatch
So stretch your legs, run
To the cliffs so high you'd need wings to jump
Let not these bodies embezzle your minds of thump thump thump
-ing bare feet through mossy forest floors
And be not chained behind closed doors

Today

Today is fun
Today is practice

Today we practice how to kill

Today we know it so well
Today we are brothers shooting
Today we are brothers talking
Today we are brothers who know

Killing isn't fun

Today is fun
Today we get better
Today we learn something new
Today we hope like every other day that
Today will be the last day we practice

Killing isn't fun

Today is fun.

Future Memories

Footsteps on dying grass
Mark future memories
Perusing our property
On mundane Monday mornings
The incessant breeze marking pieces of my soul
With chilled winter memories
Giving cool air to my lungs
Red tinge to my nose
This air invigorates me
This cool air through matted hair
Longing for wash after being awake all these days
Air sucking the energy from my skin
Only to be replaced again by the fire it itself
Has started inside

Stand-in

> These brown brick alleys
>
> Stand in for
>
> Red stone valleys

Smelly Feet

Your smelly feet
Stink up the tent
I'd rather this
Than paying rent
I much prefer
This time spent
With stinky feet
In smelly tent

30 June

We need this connection to nature

The dirt on our pants

The grass blades

Intermingling with the hairs on our legs

And the breeze making tree limbs dance

If we'd slow down

Our brains would have a chance

A Blued Ridge

                    like whales' arch'd backs

                    these hills become mountains

                    diving at distance

                    returning to the fog sea

                    as if only for mine

                    blesséd eyes to see

Living Room Lighting

Come, sit
We've run out of chairs
But there's room on the floor
We're glad you've come
Let us tell you more of the
    Love of our God
Under incandescent lighting
Let us show you more of the
    Goodness of our God
On cheap carpeting with bare feet
Let us give you more of our
    hearts and time
With warm coffee and candlelight
This can end at nine or go all night
We'll find the answers here in the Word
We'll see our God display His Might
We'll make sure every voice is heard
Lifting up all in prayer
We'll see our God move here, in this living room full of followers
We'll Love God here, in the home of the Lord

Edelweiss

Cooled but not crisp

Friday morning mountain air

With windows cracked

Trunk full of bags packed

Eyes filled by roads passed under tire

Trails passed under foot

Feet climbed, one after the other

To see cliffs and rocks stacked

Flowers picked

The altitude kills lungs and

The airborne lives on

Late Summer

The smell of wet cottonwoods

on soaked dead grass

in the late summer.

Checking the Mail

The still air says nothing

But reminds me of you

No breeze

The soft smell of asphalt

And mid-September morning

A dachshund runs up for a friendly sniff

And returns promptly satisfied

2 letters and 1 postcard from the friend

who's address changes every month

Regaling of the trails he's ventured and the towns he loved,

Asking for inflationary prices to be factored into the scale

Of bread and eggs

Chasing the Sunset

Chasing the sunset

However many thousand feet up

He reminds me I haven't been alone for a single step

The cloud floor we soar above begins to break

I am swallowed up in love

it seems more than I can take

Dreams, visions, months and years in reaching their fruition

Swathe me in love

Encompass me in joy

Encircle me in the Father's Love

Underfoot

Golden, unadulterated sunlight
coming through the shades
through the untinted, unwashed car windows
painting you
as you were meant to be
as you've always been
as I needed
as I've always needed

       Thousands of miles underfoot, now

every sunrise
every ray of every sunset
every beam slicing the clouds and canopy is you
painted on the forest floor
the soaring, jagged, snow-capped mountains
pure and golden
as you were meant to be
as you've always been

I believe that I shall look upon the goodness of the Lord
in the land of the living!
Wait for the Lord;
be strong, and let your heart take courage;
wait for the Lord!

Psalm 27:13-14 (ESV)